SONGWRITING
FOR KIDS

This Book Belongs To:

_____

_____

_____

_____

CONTENTS

Introduction

Hello, Future Songwriter!

Have you ever had a song stuck in your head? Do you feel like there is a story inside of you just waiting to burst out into a song? Well, you're in the right place! This book is your personal guide to creating your very own songs— from writing catchy lyrics to dreaming up unforgettable tunes.

What Is Songwriting?

Songwriting is a superpower! It's like telling a story but with music. A song can be about anything you want—it can make people smile, laugh, dance, or even feel inspired. You don't need to know everything about music to get started. All you need is your imagination and the desire to create something amazing.

Why You're Already a Songwriter

 That's right! You've probably already started writing songs without even knowing it. Have you ever hummed a little tune to yourself, or made up silly lyrics while walking home? That's songwriting! This book will help you take those ideas and turn them into songs that you can share with your friends and family, or even the whole world.

How to Use This Book

This book is here to help you step-by-step. We'll start by thinking about the things that inspire you—your favorite songs, what you like about them, and where you can find ideas for your own songs. Then, we'll learn how to write lyrics, how to make words rhyme, and how to create the parts of a song that people will want to sing over and over again.

TIP: Guess What?

There are no wrong answers in songwriting! Every idea you have is a good one, because it comes from YOU.

So, be brave, try new things, and remember to have fun along the way.

Your Songwriting Adventure Begins Now!

Grab a pencil, a comfy spot, and get ready to explore the world of writing your very own songs.

Whether you want to write about adventures, friendships, dreams, or even pizza (yep, that works too!), this book is here to guide you.

Let your imagination fly as you discover the awesome power of your own creativity.

Ready to make some music? Let's go!

Your Imagination is Your Greatest Instrument.

Chapter 1

Inspiration

Pronunciation: in-spuh-RAY-shun

Definition: Inspiration is when something makes you excited to create or do something new.

 **Finding Your Inspiration**

Every song has a beginning, and that beginning is called inspiration! Songs can come from just about anywhere—an exciting adventure, a favorite place, a person you love, or even something funny that happened at school. What makes songs so special is that they can capture the feelings, stories, and thoughts you have in your mind and heart.

Where Do Songs Come From?

Songs come from what we experience and feel every day. Think about the times you've been really happy, or the times you've had something on your mind that you couldn't stop thinking about. Those are the moments where songs are born.

What Did You Think About First?

Here are some places you might find inspiration for your songs.

Your Life

Think about your day-to-day life. Maybe there's something fun or exciting that's happening in your world. Your birthday, playing with your pet, or going on a trip with your family could all be great song ideas!

Your Imagination

Sometimes, the best songs come from your imagination. What if you were an astronaut flying through space? What if your dog could talk? These wild ideas can turn into fun and creative songs.

Your Feelings

Songs are also a way to talk about how you feel. Are you feeling happy, excited, or even a little nervous? Songs can help you express those emotions in a way that feels good to sing about.

Nature & The World Around You

Do you ever notice how cool it feels to walk outside on a sunny day or how peaceful it is when the rain falls? Nature is full of inspiration. The sound of birds, the feeling of the wind, or the colors of a sunset could spark an amazing song!

Exercise: What's On Your Mind?

Let's start by thinking about what's going on in your world. Here's an easy exercise to help you find inspiration for your first song.

1. Think of 5 Things You Love

On the next page, write down five things that you really enjoy. It could be a person, a place, a thing, or even a feeling.

2. Pick Your Favorite

Now, circle your favorite one on the list. This is going to be the topic of your first song!

For example, let's say you love rollercoasters. Now you've got the start of a song. We could call it *"A Wild Ride!"*

3. Write a Few Lines About It

Write down a few sentences or phrases about that thing you selected. Don't worry about writing them with rhyme or rhythm yet, just write what comes to mind.

For example: *"I love the way my stomach flips when we zoom down the track."*

"The wind in my face makes me feel like I'm flying."

5 Things I LOVE

1. _____

2. _____

3. _____

4. _____

5. _____

☆ **My Favorite is:**

_____

A Few Thoughts About My Favorite Thing:

_____

_____

_____

_____

_____

_____

_____

Activity: Inspiration All Around

Take a few minutes to look around you. What do you see? What do you hear?

Songs can come from the smallest things, like the sound of leaves rustling or the feeling of jumping in a big pile of pillows!

Here's a fun activity to get your creativity flowing:

Take a Walk: Go outside (or walk around your house if you can't go out). Look and listen carefully. Do you see something that makes you smile? Hear a sound that makes you want to dance?

Pick Your Inspiration: Write down one thing you noticed. Maybe it's the sound of birds chirping or the way the sun feels on your face.

_____

_____

_____

_____

_____

_____

_____

_____

_____

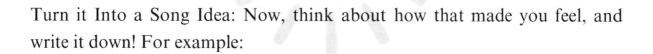

Turn it Into a Song Idea: Now, think about how that made you feel, and write it down! For example:

"The sun on my face makes me feel so warm and happy."
"The birds in the trees are singing a song, and I want to sing along!"

This is your first step toward writing your own song—finding something that speaks to you and turning it into words. Before you know it, you'll have the inspiration you need to start creating your own music!

Chapter 2

Writing Lyrics

Writing Lyrics: Telling Your Story

Now that you've found your inspiration, it's time to start turning those ideas into something magical—lyrics! Lyrics are super important because they tell a story, share your feelings, or even make people laugh and dance. Writing lyrics is like being a storyteller, but instead of just using sentences, you get to use rhythm and rhyme too!

What Are Lyrics?

Lyrics are the words you sing! They are the words that carry the message of your song. They can be short and sweet or long and detailed, depending on what you want to say. Sometimes lyrics rhyme, sometimes they don't, and sometimes they tell a story that takes the listener on an adventure! The great thing about writing lyrics is that they can be about anything you want.

Want to write about your best friend?

You Can!

Have a fun idea about a magical kingdom?

That Works Too!

Want to share how you feel on a rainy day?

Perfect!

No matter what your song is about,

lyrics are the key to making your song yours.

Exercise:
Start Simple

Before you dive into writing a whole song, let's take it one step at a time. We're going to start simple and build from there.

Pick Your Song Inspiration

Look back at the list of things that inspire you. Pick one of those topics. That's going to be what your song is about.

Write Down 3 Sentences

Now, write three simple sentences about that topic. Let's pretend your inspiration is "Helping Others."

Example Sentences:

"I helped my neighbor carry her groceries inside."

"It feels good when I can make someone smile."

"Even small acts of kindness can make a big difference."

These sentences don't have to rhyme yet!

Just focus on writing down your thoughts about your topic.

My Inspiration is: _____

Sentences About My Song Inspiration:

Turn Your Sentences Into Lyrics

Now that you have your sentences, we're going to make them a little more fun and musical. Let's turn those sentences into lyrics that feel like rhythm of a song.

Play With the Words

 You don't have to use big, fancy words to write good lyrics. Just be yourself! But here's a trick—try to add details that make your lyrics more exciting.

Instead of saying: *"I helped my neighbor carry her groceries inside."*

You could say: *"Carrying bags, lending a hand, feels like a win."*

See how it gives a little more life to the idea? You're still telling the same story, but with words that are fun to sing! Maybe your second sentence could be:

"A smile's like sunshine—makes you feel great inside."

Repeat the Important Part

A lot of songs have a part that repeats (that's usually the chorus). What's the most important part of your song? Maybe it's that you are feeling great inside. If so, you can say that again:

"A smile's like sunshine—makes you feel great inside,

(*repeat) makes you feel great inside."

Now you've got some lyrics that are starting to sound like a song!

> **TIP:**   Keep it Short and Sweet: Lyrics don't have to be long. In fact, some of the best lyrics are only a few words! Think about what you really want to say and why.

Making Sentences Sound More

EXCITING

When you're writing a song, **how** you say something can make all the difference. A sentence that's just okay can turn into something amazing with the right words!

Just like we can add beautiful colors to a painting to make it more interesting, we can add more descriptive words to our writing. Let's look at how we can take simple sentences and make them more song-like by adding adjectives and adverbs to paint a more vivid picture.

Example 1: The sky is blue.
Exciting: *The bright blue sky is shining like a painting in the clouds.*

Example 2: The dog is running.
Exciting: *The playful dog is racing quickly across the open field, his tail wagging wildly.*

Example 3: The rain is falling.
Exciting: *The gentle rain is softly dancing on the rooftops, making the world shimmer.*

Example 3: The sun is shining.
Exciting: *The golden sun is shining brightly, spreading energy like cheers from a crowd.*

Transform Your Sentences!

Now that you know what makes sentences sound more exciting, let's practice! Below are some simple sentences. Your job is to rewrite them to make them more creative, just like we did in the examples. Use descriptive words to really bring your sentences to life!

Step 1: Read the Simple Sentences

Step 2: Add Exciting Words to Make Them More Interesting

Think about how you can make these sentences more interesting. Use your five senses to describe how things look, feel, smell, taste, and sound to paint a picture in the reader's mind.

Now It's Your Turn! Rewrite the sentences below, using what you have learned:

The cookies are baking. _____

_____

_____

The car is fast. _____

_____

_____

By practicing turning simple sentences into more exciting ones, you'll learn how to make your song lyrics more powerful and expressive. Have fun and let your imagination run wild!

Activity: Paint a Picture with Your Words

Lyrics are a bit like painting a picture with words. When you write a song, you want your listeners to be able to imagine exactly what you're singing about. So let's practice "painting" with words!

Think About Your Topic: Picture it in your mind.

What do you see? What do you feel? What can you smell or hear? Write down some words that describe those things.

For Example:

Topic: A Rainy Day

Describing Words: wet, grey, puddles, cold, splashing, drip, thunder

Use Those Words in Your Lyrics

Now take some of those descriptive words and turn them into lyrics. Try writing a short verse about the rain:

> *"The rain is falling, splashing all around,*
>
> *Grey skies above me, puddles on the ground."*

See how the words help you picture the rain? You can do this with anything—your dog, a holiday, a baseball game—and make your lyrics more interesting.

My Inspiration is:

_____

Words that Describe My Topic:

_____   _____   _____

_____   _____   _____

_____   _____   _____

_____   _____   _____

_____   _____   _____

_____   _____   _____

Lyrics Using My Descriptive Words

_____

_____

_____

_____

_____

_____

_____

_____

_____

_____

_____

_____

_____

_____

My Inspiration is:

_____

Words that Describe My Topic:

_____   _____   _____

_____   _____   _____

_____   _____   _____

_____   _____   _____

_____   _____   _____

_____   _____   _____

Lyrics Using My Descriptive Words

_____

_____

_____

_____

_____

_____

_____

_____

_____

_____

_____

_____

_____

DON'T FORGET!

Tips for Writing Great Lyrics

Be Yourself

Don't try to use big words if that's not how you talk.

Your lyrics should sound like you!

Keep it Simple

Sometimes the simplest words make the best songs.

Have Fun!

Writing lyrics is like playing with words.

Don't worry if it's perfect—just enjoy creating your song!

Remember, songs come from your heart, so write about what matters to you. Whether it's something funny, something serious, or something in between, your lyrics are a way to share your voice with the world.

Rhyming

Rhyming & Word Play: Making Your Lyrics Catchy

You've started writing your lyrics, and they're already sounding awesome! Now, let's make them even more fun by adding some rhymes and a little more word play. Rhymes are a great way to make your song catchy—they're what get 'stuck' in people's heads and make them want to sing along!

What is a Rhyme?

A rhyme happens when two words sound the same at the end. Think of words like cat and hat, or blue and you. When you put words like these at the end of your lines, they *create a rhythm* that feels fun to sing and easy to remember.

Rhyme:
moon
tune

Imagine singing this:

"The sky is so blue, and I'm thinking of you."

The rhyme makes the words flow together like a little dance, and that's what keeps listeners hooked!

How Do Rhymes Help Your Song?

Rhymes are like the glue that holds your lyrics together. *They help create a rhythm* that's fun to sing and make your lyrics sound smoother. Rhyming can also add a playful twist to your song—especially when you get creative with the words you choose!

Flower, Power
Sunny, Funny
Where, Chair
Shining, Climbing

Exercise:
Rhyming Practice

Let's practice rhyming! I'll give you a word, and your job is to find a word or words that rhyme with it. Here are a few examples of rhyming words to get you started:

Today, Play, Stay

Fun, Run, Sun

Each note below contains a word. Take a look at the example below. See how many words you can rhyme and write them inside the notes.

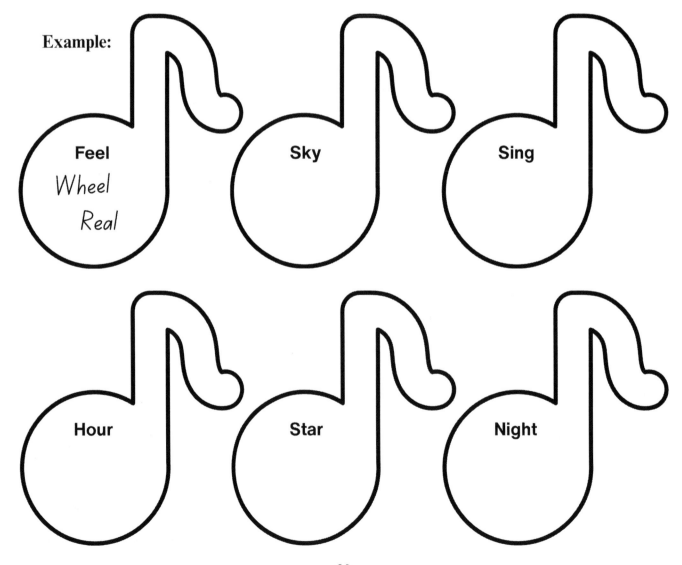

Example:

Feel — *Wheel, Real*

Sky

Sing

Hour

Star

Night

Great! Now, Let's look at an example of lyrics using **Rhyming Pairs**.

We will use: *Today, Play Stay*

Here are two lines of lyrics using those rhyming word sets:

"The sun is shining bright today,
I want to go outside and play."

We have written a rhyming line! It's that simple. Now it's your turn. You can do this with any words you like to make your song catchy.

Use can use the lyrics you started on pages 26-27. Write your rhyming lines here:

_____

_____

_____

_____

_____

_____

_____

_____

_____

_____

_____

_____

_____

_____

What Happens If You Can't Find a Rhyme?

Don't worry! Not every line in your song has to rhyme. Some of the best songs mix rhyming lines with ones that don't rhyme at all. If you can't find a word that rhymes, you can always try these tricks:

Use Near Rhymes

Sometimes, words don't rhyme perfectly, but they sound similar enough.

For example (say these words out loud):

Home and **Alone**

Time and **Shine**

These words don't match exactly, but they still sound good together!

Switch the Word Order

If you can't find a rhyme, try switching your sentence around to make it easier to rhyme. For example, your line may be: *"I can't wait to hang out with my friends."*

If you can't find a rhyme, try switching the word order:

"Hanging out with friends is always a blast."

Now you have more options like "fast" or "last" to rhyme with "blast."

Example rhyme: *"Hanging out with friends is always a blast, making memories that will last."*

Activity: Fill in the Rhymes

Let's have some fun with rhyming by filling in the blanks! I'll give you the first part of a line, and you'll create your own rhyme to finish it. Ready?

Grab your pencil to finish these lines, and see what creative rhymes you come up with!

"When the stars come out, I..."

_____

_____

_____

"The snow is falling on the..."

_____

_____

_____

"I can't wait to go and..."

_____

_____

_____

"I see the rainbow in the..."

_____

_____

_____

Playing with Words: Add Some Fun!

Rhyming isn't the only way to make your lyrics catchy. You can also play around with the way words sound and repeat certain phrases to make your song stick in people's minds. Here are a few ways to have some fun with words:

☑ **Alliteration (Pronounced: uh-lit-uh-RAY-shuhn)**

Alliteration is when you use the same letter or sound at the beginning of words that are close together, like this:

"Silly snakes slither softly." (All the words start with the letter 'S')

"Bouncing bunnies bravely build big bridges." (Notice the letter 'B')

Try using alliteration in your song for a fun effect. It can make your lyrics sound smooth and memorable!

☑ **Repeating Lines**

Some of the best songs repeat certain lines or phrases. If there's something important in your song, don't be afraid to say it again!

For example: *"I'll always be your friend, I'll always be your friend."*

Repeating the most important part helps it stick in people's minds.

☑ **Rhythm and Rhyme Together**

Rhyming works best when you also have a strong rhythm. Clap along with your lyrics as you sing them. Does the rhythm feel right? Try changing the number of words in each line to match the beat.

Similes & Metaphors: Songwriting Magic

☑ Simile
(Pronounced: SIM-uh-lee)

When your write creatively, **similes** compare two things using "like" or "as" to create a vivid picture for the listener. They help make emotions and experiences easier to understand.

For Example: "The melody floated through the air like a feather" helps you imagine something light, gentle, and easy to follow.

Use a Simile to Complete These Lines:

His laugh was as loud as _____.

The music flowed like _____.

☑ Metaphor
(Pronounced: MET-uh-for)

Metaphors compare two unlike things by giving the qualities of one to the other. This helps your listener imagine something in a new way.

For Example: "My heart is a drum" compares a heart to a drum, making you think of strong beats or rhythm, even though a heart and drum are different.

Use a Metaphor to Complete These Lines:

The stars are a _____.

Her smile is a _____.

Exercise:
Create a Rhyming Chorus

Now that you've practiced rhyming, let's write a chorus! The chorus is usually the catchiest part of the song that is repeated several times, and it often uses rhymes to make it easy to sing along:

Here's a simple way to start:

Pick one idea from your song. Write a few lines that rhyme and describe your idea. Here is an example using the rollercoaster inspiration:

> *"Click-clack up the track, we're climbing up so high,*
>
> *Hands in the air, we're reaching for the sky.*
>
> *Heart's racing fast, can't wait for the drop,*
>
> *We'll be laughing and screaming until the ride stops!"*

Sing it out loud! Does it feel catchy? If so, great! If not, try switching a word or changing the rhyme until it feels right.

Rhyming and word play can take your song to the next level by making it fun, playful, and easy to sing along with. So go ahead—try out different rhymes, play with the way your words sound, and create a song that everyone will want to sing!

My Inspiration is:

_____

Words and Rhymes that Describe My Topic:

_____   _____   _____

_____   _____   _____

_____   _____   _____

_____   _____   _____

_____   _____   _____

_____   _____   _____

My Rhyming Chorus:

_____

_____

_____

_____

_____

_____

_____

_____

_____

_____

_____

_____

Chapter 3
Song Structure

Sections of a Song: The Building Blocks of Music

Every song you hear has parts, or sections, that work together like pieces of a puzzle to make the whole song feel complete. These sections help tell the story of your song, and each one has a special job to do.

 Let's break it down:

Verse:

This is where your story happens! In the verses, you're setting the scene and giving your listeners all the details. It's like the part of a movie where the action starts. Each verse tells more of the story, with new words each time.

Example: If your song is about going on an adventure, the verses could describe where you're going, what you see, or how you feel.

Chorus:

The chorus is the heart of the song—the part that everyone remembers and sings along to. It's usually repeated several times and has the same words and melody each time it comes around. The chorus is your chance to make a big statement!

Example: In our adventure song, the chorus might be:

"*Let's go somewhere, let's take a ride, Adventure's waiting just outside.*"

It's the part that sticks in people's heads long after the song is over.

Bridge:

Think of the bridge like a plot twist. It's a section that sounds different from the verse and chorus, giving your song a little surprise before bringing it back to the familiar chorus. The bridge often adds new emotions or ideas to the song. It can be a different feeling or an unexpected change in the story.

Example: Maybe in the bridge, you realize that the adventure may not always go as planned, and the lyrics show how you feel about it.

> *"Lost or found, it's all the same,*
> *Every journey's part of the game.*
> *We make new stories every mile,*
> *And every stop brings one more smile."*

Why Song Structure Matters

Without sections like verses and choruses, songs could feel a little messy, like trying to build a castle with no plan. Song structure helps your song flow smoothly from one part to the next, keeping your listeners interested and excited. By having these different parts work together, your song tells a full story and takes people on a journey with you.

So, next time you write a song, think about these building blocks. They'll help you shape your ideas into something amazing—and make your song one that people can't stop singing!

Exercise:
Building Your Song Structure

Now that you know about the different parts of a song,

let's try putting them together!

Get Your Song Inspiration:

Look back at your inspirations and lyrics from earlier. Choose one idea you want to build a song around (like your favorite adventure, a fun memory, or a feeling).

My inspiration is:_____

Write Verse 1:

Start by telling your story in the verse. Describe what's happening or how you feel. Here's an example for a song about making new friends:

"A little bit nervous, a little bit shy, But I say "hello" and give it a try.

We start to talk, and just like that, We're laughing together, how cool is that?"

Start With Words and Rhymes that Describe Your Topic:

_____	_____	_____
_____	_____	_____
_____	_____	_____
_____	_____	_____
_____	_____	_____
_____	_____	_____

Start your first verse here. Don't forget your descriptive and exciting words!

Create a Chorus:

Now, write a chorus that sums up your main idea. Remember, the chorus is usually the part that repeats, so keep it simple and catchy. Here's a chorus example for our friendship song:

"New friends, new adventures,
Side by side, the fun just gets better.
Every high-five, every game we play,
It feels so good to make a friend today!"

Add a Second Verse: In the second verse, tell more of the story.

What else happens? How do you feel? Why?

Here is a second verse that tells more of the story in our sample song.

"Different ideas, but that's okay, We learn new things along the way.

It's not just fun, it's something more—A friendship opens a brand-new door."

_____

_____

_____

_____

_____

_____

_____

_____

_____

_____

_____

_____

_____

_____

_____

_____

_____

_____

_____

_____

Optional: Add a Bridge

If you're feeling adventurous, try adding a bridge to change things up. Maybe it's a quieter or more exciting part of your song. Here's a bridge example that talks more about the *feeling* of friendship:

"When I reach out, the world feels wide, And friends make life an awesome ride.

Every new face can bring a surprise, And friendships grow right before our eyes."

_____

_____

_____

_____

_____

_____

_____

_____

_____

_____

_____

_____

_____

_____

_____

_____

_____

_____

Put It All Together:

Now you've got the parts of your song—two verses, a chorus, and maybe even a bridge. Sing them in this order:

Verse 1, Chorus, Verse 2, Chorus, (Optional Bridge), Chorus

Verse 1: _____

_____

_____

_____

Chorus: _____

_____

_____

_____

Verse 2: _____

_____

_____

_____

Chorus: _____

_____

_____

_____

Bridge (optional): _____

_____

_____

_____

Chorus: _____

_____

_____

_____

You've just written a song using song structure! By fitting these pieces together, you've created something fun and easy for listeners to follow. Keep practicing with different topics, and soon, you'll be writing songs with awesome structure every time!

Up Next: Melody

A melody gives your song its unique sound, making it memorable and fun to sing. In the next chapter, we'll explore how to create a tune that fits your lyrics and expresses the emotions behind your words. Let's dive into the world of melodies and discover how music can help tell your story!

The Melody is Already Inside You.

Let it Out and

Watch it Grow!

Chapter 4

Melody

Creating a Melody

Now that you've started writing some awesome lyrics, it's time to bring them to life with a melody! But what is a melody, you ask? Think of a melody as the tune of the song—the part that you can't help but hum or sing over and over again. It's like the voice of your song!

You already know more about melodies than you think! Have you ever gotten a song stuck in your head? That's because the melody was so catchy, your brain just couldn't let it go.

Where Do Melodies Come From?

Here's the fun part: melodies can come from anywhere! You can hum one while brushing your teeth, or a tune might pop into your head while you're playing outside. You don't need a piano or any instruments to make a melody—your voice is your best tool!

Sometimes, the melody comes from how your lyrics sound. Try reading your lyrics out loud. Do the words feel like they want to be sung in a high voice or a low one? Fast or slow? That's the beginning of your melody!

How to Build Your Melody

Building a melody is like creating a path for your song to walk along.

Here's how to get started:

Start Simple: Hum a few notes that feel good to you. Don't worry if it's perfect—just let the notes come out naturally. You can start with just a couple of notes that repeat, or go up and down like a staircase.

Match Your Melody to Your Words:

Now try singing the first line of your lyrics with the melody you hummed. Does it sound good? Does it feel like the words and the melody are friends? If not, no worries—try changing the notes a little until it feels right!

Make It Memorable:

Think about some of your favorite songs. What's the part that sticks in your head the most? That's usually the chorus! To make your melody memorable, try repeating some notes in the chorus so that everyone can sing along.

Melody Trick: Highs and Lows

Every great melody has some highs and lows. Imagine your melody is a rollercoaster ride—sometimes it goes up high, and sometimes it swoops down low. This makes your song exciting and fun to listen to!

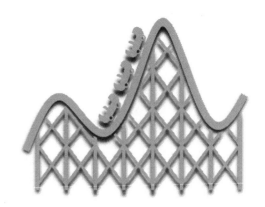

Try singing some of your lyrics using higher notes, and then mix in some lower notes. Play around with it until you find the combination that feels just right.

Hum It, Sing It, Play It!

Once you've found a melody you like, try singing it a few times. Can you remember it without looking at your lyrics? If you can, awesome! You've just created your melody. If you have an instrument like a piano or guitar, you can even try playing your melody on it. But if not, no problem—your voice is all you need!

> **TIP:** Melodies don't have to be complicated.
> Some of the best songs have really simple melodies that are easy to remember.

Your Turn!

Now it's your turn to create a melody for the song you're working on. Start by humming or singing your lyrics, then try out different notes until something feels just right.* Don't be afraid to experiment, and most importantly—have fun!

If you already know how to write music notes on the staff or guitar chords, here is a page with space to get started writing your melody. If you do not yet write music notation, this space can be used to write more of your amazing lyrics...

Song Title:

Chapter 5

Rhythm & Flow

Rhythm: Bringing Your Song to Life

Now that you've got your melody, lyrics, and the parts of your song figured out, it's time to add something extra special—rhythm! Rhythm is what gives your song its pulse, or beat. It's what makes your song move and feel alive.

What is Rhythm?

Rhythm is the pattern of beats in a song. Imagine clapping your hands to a song on the radio or tapping your foot to the beat. That's rhythm! It's what helps your lyrics flow smoothly and keeps your song moving forward.

- Some songs have fast rhythms, like when you're running or jumping.

- Other songs have slow rhythms, like when you're walking or swaying.

How Rhythm Makes Your Song Move

Every song has a rhythm that keeps everything in time. Think about the beat of your favorite song—whether it's fast and makes you want to dance, or slow and makes you feel relaxed, that's the rhythm at work. The cool thing is, you get to decide what the rhythm of your song will be!

What Songs Make You Want to Dance?

Play one of the songs now, and listen for the rhythm. What do you hear that creates the beat in the song? Is it the instruments? Do the words have a strong rhythm pattern?

How Rhythm Works with Your Lyrics and Melody

Now that you've written your lyrics and melody, rhythm will help tie them together. Think of rhythm like a glue that holds everything in place. Your words and melody need a beat to flow smoothly, and that's where rhythm comes in.

Let's practice with this line:

"The stars are shining in the sky, I'm dreaming as they pass me by."

Now, try tapping or clapping along with the words. Feel how some words take more time, while others are shorter? That's the rhythm starting to form!

Fast Rhythm:

If your song is energetic or exciting (like a sunny day or an adventure), it might have a faster beat.

Example: Think of a song that feels like running or jumping. The rhythm will be quick, and your lyrics will match that speed!

Slow Rhythm:

If your song is calm or thoughtful (like a rainy day or a quiet moment), the beat might be slower.

Example: A slow rhythm might feel like walking slowly or swaying back and forth. The lyrics will flow gently with the beat.

Rhythm Trick: Fast vs. Slow

The speed of your song is called **tempo**. Changing the tempo can change the whole feeling of your song! Here's how to experiment with tempo:

Start Slow: Sing one of your verses slowly. How does it make you feel? Does it sound calm or peaceful?

Speed It Up: Now sing the same verse quickly. Does it sound more exciting? Does it make you want to dance?

Pick Your Tempo: Decide how fast or slow you want your song to be. Think about how you want people to feel when they hear it. Fast songs are full of energy, while slow songs are more relaxed. Choose the tempo that fits your song's mood.

Exercise: Clap it Out!

To really understand how rhythm works,
let's start by clapping the beat of your song.

Follow these steps:

Choose a Verse or Chorus: Pick one part of your song that you want to work with.

Clap to the Beat: As you say your lyrics out loud, try clapping your hands to the beat. Does the rhythm feel fast or slow? Is it steady? Keep clapping and see if your lyrics match the beat.

> **TIP:** Clap once for each word, or for each syllable if your words are longer. You'll notice that some words need more claps, like "shin-ing". Others only need one clap, like "sky".

Adjust the Rhythm: If your words don't fit the beat, you can change the rhythm or the words to make it flow better. Try adding an extra beat or changing the speed of your claps until everything feels just right.

What is Flow?

Once you've got your rhythm, you'll notice that the song starts to flow. Flow is how smoothly your lyrics, melody, and rhythm fit together. It's like riding a bike—you want everything to move along easily without feeling like you're hitting bumps along the way.

Here's how to keep your song flowing:

- **Keep the Beat Steady:** Make sure the rhythm stays even, like a steady heartbeat, throughout your song.

- **Watch for Too Many Words:** If there are too many words in a line, it can make the rhythm feel bumpy. Try shortening a line or breaking it into two if the rhythm doesn't feel quite right.

- **Practice Singing:** Sing your lyrics out loud with your melody and the rhythm. Does it feel smooth and natural? If something feels tricky, try changing the words or melody until it flows better.

Activity: Stomp, Clap, and Tap

Let's get moving with some rhythm fun! You're going to use your body to create the beat for your song.

1. **Pick a Part of Your Song:** Work on the parts of your song one section at at time.

2. **Stomp the Beat:** Start by stomping your feet to make the beat. If your song is fast, stomp quickly. If it's slow, stomp slowly. Feel how the rhythm makes your song come to life!

3. **Clap Along:** Now, add some claps! Clap your hands to match the rhythm of your lyrics. Do you notice how the rhythm and words fit together like pieces of a puzzle?

4. **Tap to the Flow:** Finally, try tapping your hands on your lap, a table, or even tap a pencil to the beat. Let the rhythm flow through your body. The more you tap and stomp, the more you'll feel the rhythm guiding your song.

Now that you've got an understanding of rhythm and flow, you're turning your song into something that people can't help but move to. The beat is what will keep your listeners connected to the song and make it unforgettable. So go ahead, find your rhythm, and watch your song come alive!

Chapter 6

Putting it All Together

You've made it! You've learned how to find inspiration, write lyrics, create a melody, build a song structure, and add rhythm and flow. Now it's time to put everything together and create your very own song from start to finish. This is the exciting part—where all the pieces come together, like making a puzzle where every part fits just right!

Step 1: Start with Your Idea

Remember how we talked about finding inspiration? Every great song starts with an idea. It could be something that happened to you, a place you love, a person who makes you smile, or even something from your imagination. Before you start writing your song, think about what message or feeling you want to share.

What's your song about? Maybe it's a feeling,

a happy memory, or a fun moment with a friend.

My Inspiration is:

_____

My Description and Rhyming Words:

_____	_____	_____
_____	_____	_____
_____	_____	_____
_____	_____	_____
_____	_____	_____

Sentences and Rhymes Using My Descriptive Words:

_____

_____

_____

_____

_____

_____

_____

_____

_____

_____

_____

Step 2: Write Your Lyrics

Now that you have your idea, it's time to start writing the lyrics. Think about the story you want to tell, and write it down in words remembering your song structure (Verse 1, Chorus, Verse 2, Chorus, optional Bridge, Chorus). You don't have to rhyme every line, but try to use rhymes when it feels right. Here's a reminder of the steps for writing lyrics with an example song about the beach:

Verse: This is where your story starts. What happens first? What do you want to say or describe? Each verse will be a new part of your story.

Example Verse 1:

"Sun on my face, toes in the sand,
Shells in my pocket, treasures in hand.
Waves crash and tumble, singing their tune,
I dance with the tide all afternoon."

Example Verse 2:

"Seagulls are calling, high in the sky,
Surfboards glide as dolphins swim by.
Building castles, towers so tall,
Watch as the ocean swallows them all."

Chorus: The chorus is the part that repeats. It's the heart of your song—the part that people will remember and sing along to.

Example Chorus: *"Ride the waves, feel the breeze,*
Ocean whispers through the seas.
Splash and swim, laugh and play,
It's a perfect beachy day!"

Bridge (Optional): The bridge adds something new to your song, like a twist or a change in the story. It's usually a little different from the verses and chorus.

Example Bridge: *"Even when the sun sinks low,*
And stars appear with a gentle glow,
The sound of waves will always stay,
Bringing me back to this ocean day."

Verse 1

Verse 2

Chorus

Bridge

Step 3: Add Your Melody

You've got your lyrics, and now it's time to sing them! Every great song needs a melody, and the melody is like the voice of your song. Here's how you can add your melody:

1. **Hum the Tune:** Start by humming the first verse of your lyrics. What does it sound like? Does it want to be a high note or a low one? Play around with different notes until it feels just right.

2. **Sing Your Chorus:** The chorus should be the catchiest part of your song, so make sure your melody repeats here. Try singing the chorus a few times until you find a tune that feels fun and easy to remember.

3. **Practice the Flow:** Sing your whole song from start to finish. Does the melody flow smoothly from the verse to the chorus? Adjust any parts that feel tricky.

Step 4: Check the Rhythm & Flow

Now that you've got your lyrics and melody, it's time to add the rhythm that will make your song really come to life. Clap, stomp, or tap along as you sing to make sure your song has a steady beat. Ask yourself:

- Does the rhythm fit the mood of your song?

- Is it fast and fun, or slow and peaceful?

- Do the words match the beat? If a line feels rushed, try adding a pause or changing a word to make it flow better.

Here's a quick way to practice:

- Clap along to the beat while you sing your song.

- If a word feels out of place, change it to fit the rhythm.

- Keep repeating until everything flows smoothly!

Step 5: Put It All Together!

Now that you have your lyrics, melody, and rhythm, it's time to put the whole song together! Here's a step-by-step review to put all the pieces in place:

1. **Sing the Verse:** Start by singing your first verse. Tell your story clearly and keep the rhythm steady.

2. **Move into the Chorus:** After the verse, jump into your chorus. Make sure the chorus feels big and catchy, something that people will want to sing along with.

3. **Add More Verses:** If your song has more than one verse, keep telling the story. Each verse can add new details or move the story forward.

4. **Optional - Add a Bridge:** If you've written a bridge, sing that part after your second chorus to add something new to your song.

5. **End with the Chorus:** Most songs end with the chorus because it's the part people remember the most. Sing your chorus one last time to wrap up your song.

Practice Makes Perfect!

Now that you've put all the pieces together, sing your song a few times from start to finish. How does it feel? Does it tell the story you want to share? Does the melody feel right? The more you practice, the smoother it will get.

Don't worry if you need to make a few changes—that's part of the fun! Every songwriter makes changes to their songs until everything feels just right.

Chapter 7

Review and Revision: Making Your Songs Even Better

Now that you've written your song, guess what? Your job as a songwriter isn't finished yet! Every great songwriter goes back to review and revise their songs, making little changes that help the song flow better, sound stronger, or express feelings more clearly. Revising your song doesn't mean you did something wrong —it just means you're making it the best it can be!

What Is Revision?

Revision is when you go back to what you've already written and look for places where you can make improvements. It could mean changing a word to make it rhyme better, fixing the rhythm so the lyrics fit the beat, or adding a new line to make the song even more fun. Think of revision like adding the final touches to a cool drawing—it's what helps your song shine!

Why Is Revision Important?

Even the best songwriters don't get it perfect on the first try. That's why it's important to review your song and see if there are any spots where you can make it even better. When you take the time to revise, you'll notice things you didn't see the first time, and your song will be even more fun to sing!

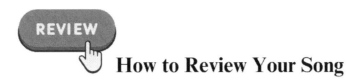

How to Review Your Song

- **Sing It Out Loud:** Sometimes, just singing your song out loud can help you hear if something sounds a little off. Maybe a line doesn't flow smoothly, or a word doesn't quite fit. When you sing it, you can spot what needs a little tweaking.

- **Check the Rhymes:** Are your rhymes working? Do they feel smooth and natural, or are they a bit forced? If a rhyme feels clunky, try swapping in a different word that sounds better.

- **Fix the Rhythm:** Clap along with your song and see if the rhythm works. Do all the words fit the beat? If not, you can change a word or add a small pause to make it flow better.

Small Changes Make a Big Difference!

Even tiny changes can make your song feel new and exciting. Don't be afraid to try something different! You might come up with a new line or a better rhyme that makes your song even more special.

Use the Next Pages for the Final Draft of Your New Song!

An Important Tip To Remember:
Revising does not mean you didn't do a great job—
it means you're making your song the best it can be!

Song Title: _____

_____

_____

_____

_____

_____

_____

_____

_____

_____

_____

_____

_____

_____

_____

_____

_____

_____

_____

_____

_____

_____

_____

_____

_____

_____

Activity: Share Your Song!

Once you've finished your song, it's time to share it with someone! You can sing it for your family, friends, or even perform it at school. Sharing your song is the best way to show off all the hard work you've done, and who knows—you might inspire someone else to write their own song too!

You've Done It!

You've learned how to find inspiration, write catchy lyrics, create a melody, add rhythm and flow, and now you've put it all together into your very own song. That's a huge achievement!

Remember, every song you write is a piece of your story, and you can keep writing more songs whenever you want. So keep dreaming, keep singing, and keep creating—because the world needs to hear your voice!

Chapter 8

Song Starters

Welcome to the Song Starters chapter! This is where your imagination can run wild. Sometimes, all it takes is a spark—just a word or a feeling—to ignite a song idea. In this section, you'll find prompts to get your creativity flowing and help you shape your own musical stories. Be confident in your ability to write amazing songs. Remember, there are no wrong ideas here, only endless possibilities!

"When I opened the door, I couldn't believe what I saw..."

Let your imagination soar! What surprising thing is waiting behind the door?

"If I could make a wish, I'd wish for..."

What would your dream wish be? How would it change your life?

"The best part of my day was when..."

Write about the happiest moment of your day and turn it into a feel-good song.

"There's a secret in the forest..."

Create a magical or mysterious story about something hidden deep in the woods.

"My pet has a double life as..."

Imagine your pet as a superhero or secret agent. What kinds of adventures do they go on?

"I was walking down the street when suddenly..."

What unexpected event or adventure happens to you on a regular day?

"If I could go anywhere in the world, I'd go to..."

Describe the sights, sounds, and feelings of your

dream destination in a song.

"The last time I saw my best friend..."

Tell a story about a fun memory with your best friend, and make it

into a song.

"The rain started to fall, but I..."

Write a song about a rainy day.

How does the rain make you feel, and what happens next?

"The stars were so bright, I felt like..."

Use the night sky as inspiration to write about a calm,

quiet moment under the stars.

"If I could be invisible for a day..."

What would you do if no one could see you? Write about your

sneaky adventures.

"My favorite holiday is..."

Write a song about your favorite holiday and why it's so special.

Include fun details like decorations, food, and activities!

"The sound of the ocean makes me feel..."

Imagine you're by the ocean. How does the sound of the

waves make you feel? What stories could you tell in a song?

"I can't stop laughing when..."

Write a funny song about something or

someone that always makes you laugh.

"If I had wings, I would fly to..."

Where would you go if you could fly?

Describe the adventure and the view from above.

"If I were a superhero, my superpower would be..."

Describe your superhero identity, your superpower, and how

you'd save the day in a song.

"At night, I dream about..."

Turn your dreams or daydreams into a creative, adventurous song.

"When I grow up, I want to be..."

Turn your dreams about the future into a song.

What kind of life do you see for yourself?

"The first day of school felt like..."

Write a song about the excitement or nervousness of starting

something new, like the first day of school.

"If I could be any animal for a day..."

What animal would you be, and what would your day look like?

"There's a magical tree that grants wishes..."

Write a song about a magical tree and the wishes

that come true when you visit it.

"In the middle of the night, I heard a strange noise..."

Write a mysterious song about what could be making that strange

noise and how you feel about it.

"My family is the best because..."

Write a song celebrating your family and

what makes them awesome.

"On a snowy day, I love to..."

Use the cold, snowy weather to inspire a song about

your favorite winter activities.

""There's a treasure map in my hand..."

Write an adventurous song about following a

treasure map and the quest to find the hidden treasure.

"The new kid at school looked scared, but I..."

Write a song about meeting someone new and becoming friends,

even if they're different from you.

"A letter arrived in the mail, and it said..."

Imagine you receive an unexpected letter. What does it say?

What happens next?

"If I had a time machine, I'd travel to..."

Write about your journey to the past or the

future. What do you see and experience?

"When the clock struck midnight..."

Write a song about something magical or unexpected

that happens at midnight.

Feeling Inspired?

Circle the Song Starters that you would like to begin with. Maybe one of these
ideas helped you think of an even better one! Use the journal pages in Chapter 10
to get started!

Every time you write,
you become a better songwriter.
Keep going,
you've got this!

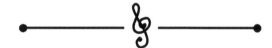

The best songs
don't have to be perfect—
they just have to be yours.

Chapter 9

Songwriting Challenges & Extra Activities

Keep Writing and Keep Creating!

With these songwriting challenges and extra activities, you can keep exploring new ideas and becoming an even better songwriter. The more you write, the more creative you'll become. So keep experimenting, keep playing, and most importantly—keep having fun with your music!

You've already learned how to write an awesome song, but the best part about being a songwriter is that there's always more to explore! Now, it's time for some songwriting challenges and fun activities that will help you keep your creativity flowing and stretch your musical muscles. These challenges are designed to make songwriting even more exciting, so grab your pencil and let's dive in!

Challenge 1: Write a Song in a New Style

You've probably heard lots of different types of music—like pop, rock, hip-hop, or country. Now it's your turn to try writing a song in a new style! Don't worry if you've never written in this style before—this is all about having fun and trying something new.

- **Pick a Style:** Choose a style of music you haven't written before. Maybe you'll try writing a hip-hop song with lots of rhythm and rhymes, a rock song with a powerful beat, or a country ballad with a slower, but rhythmic feel.

- **Write Your Lyrics:** Think about what kind of story or feeling fits this style. If you're writing a rock song, maybe it's about something exciting. If it's hip-hop, you might focus on cool rhymes and rhythm.

- **Add the Beat:** Every music style has a different rhythm. If you're writing a pop song, keep the beat steady and catchy. If you're writing country, try to tell a story that moves with the music.

Example: If you're writing a hip-hop song, your lyrics could be:

"I'm walking down the street, feel the beat under my feet,

Got my headphones on, and my music sounds so sweet!"

 Challenge 2: Write with a Friend

Sometimes the best songs come from working with someone else! This challenge is all about teaming up with a friend. Songwriting together can bring out new ideas and make the process even more fun.

- **Pick a Topic Together:** Choose something you both love. Maybe it's a game you like to play, a fun memory you have, or something you both dream about.

- **Take Turns Writing:** You can each write a line, a verse, or the chorus. One person might write the melody, and the other can work on the rhythm. Working together is a great way to combine your creative ideas!

- **Perform Your Song:** Once you've written the song, practice it together and perform it for your friends and family.

Challenge 3: The Three-Word Challenge

This challenge is a little tricky, but a lot of fun! Your goal is to write a song using three special words that you choose ahead of time. The words can be anything—colors, animals, or even random things you see around you.

- **Pick Your Three Words:** Ask a friend or family member to give you three random words. It could be something like "butterfly," "ocean," and "laugh".

- **Write Your Song:** Now, write a song that includes all three words. You can use them in any order, but they all have to be in the lyrics somewhere!

- **Challenge Yourself:** See if you can write the song in 30 minutes or less. The faster you write, the more fun and creative the challenge will be!

Example: Using the words "butterfly," "ocean," and "laugh," you could write:

"The butterfly flew by as we laughed and played,

The ocean was calling on that sunny day."

Challenge 4: Create a Song Using Only Sounds

Who says you need lyrics to make a song?

In this challenge, you'll create a song using only sounds. You can use your voice, clapping, tapping, or even things around your house to make music. This is a great way to experiment with rhythm and melody without worrying about words.

- **Find Your Instruments:** Look around your room or house. You can tap on a table, shake a jar with coins in it, or clap your hands to create sounds.

- **Create a Beat:** Start by creating a simple beat using your "instruments."

- **Add Layers:** Once you've got your beat, add more sounds. Maybe you can hum a melody or add a fun clapping pattern.

- **Record Your Song:** If you have a phone or a computer, try recording your song! You can even share it with friends and see if they can figure out what "instruments" you used.

 Challenge 5:

The Song Rewrite Super Challenge

Every songwriter knows that songs don't have to stay the same forever. In this challenge, you'll take a song you've already written and give it a remix or rewrite! This is a great way to see how your song could change and grow with new ideas.

- **Change the Tempo:** If your song is fast, try singing it slowly. Does it change the feeling of the song? How does it sound now?

- **Switch the Style:** If your song is a pop song, try turning it into a country song or a ballad. How does the melody change? What new lyrics could fit?

- **Add a New Verse or Bridge:** If your song feels short, add a new verse or bridge to make it longer. You could add a twist to the story or a surprise ending.

Bonus Activity:

Write a Song for Someone Special

Sometimes the best songs are the ones we write for someone we care about. For this activity, think about someone special in your life—your best friend, a family member, or even your pet—and write a song just for them.

- **Think About Why They're Special:** What makes this person (or pet!) so important to you? Is it something they do or a feeling they give you?
- **Write the Lyrics:** Write a verse or chorus about why they're special. Tell them how much they mean to you, or describe a fun memory you have together.
- **Sing It to Them:** Once your song is ready, sing it to the person you wrote it for! This is a great way to share your music and make someone feel amazing.

Example: If you're writing a song for your best friend, you might write:

"You're always by my side, through the good and the bad,
You make me laugh when I'm feeling sad."

Chapter 10

Journaling: A Place For Your Ideas

Songwriting Journal: Your Creative Space

Welcome to your very own Songwriting Journal! This is where your ideas, lyrics, and melodies come together in one special place. Think of this section as your creative playground—there are no rules here! You can write anything you want, whether it's a whole song, a few lines of lyrics, or even just a fun idea that pops into your head.

Why Have a Songwriting Journal?

Every songwriter, no matter how young or old, needs a place to capture their thoughts and inspirations. Your Songwriting Journal is here to help you:

- **Keep Track of Your Songs:** Write down your lyrics, melodies, and rhythms so you can always come back to them later. Sometimes the best songs start as just a few words or a little hum, and grow into something amazing!

- **Explore New Ideas:** Feel free to doodle, scribble, or jot down any random ideas that come to mind. You never know when a small thought might turn into your next great song.

- **Rewrite & Improve:** Great songwriters know that the first draft of a song is just the beginning. Use these journal pages to go back and change things if you need to. You can make your songs better by adding new lines, trying different words, or even creating a whole new melody!

What Can You Do in a Songwriting Journal?

- **Write Your Lyrics:** Use the lined pages to write down full song lyrics or just a few lines that you're working on. Whether it's the chorus of a song or a new verse, this is the perfect place to get it all down on paper.

- **Sketch Out Your Melody:** Got a tune stuck in your head? You can hum it, sing it, and now you can write it here! Use the manuscript pages to draw out your melody, just like a real composer.

- **Collect Your Ideas:** Not ready to write a whole song yet? That's okay! Use this space to gather your thoughts, brainstorm new song topics, or even draw something that inspires you.

Your Journey as a Songwriter

This journal isn't just a place for you to write songs—it's a part of your journey as a songwriter. Every page you fill is one more step toward becoming the kind of songwriter you want to be. Whether you're writing about an unexpected day, a winning game, or something that makes you feel strong emotions, every song is a piece of your story.

And remember: there's no rush! Songwriting is not a race. Some days you'll write a whole song, and other days you might just jot down a single lyric. Both are important, and they're all part of your creative process.

Your Song, Your Voice

This is *your* writing space. Everything you write here is yours, and that makes it special. You're telling your story through music, and the world needs to hear your voice. So fill these pages with your thoughts, dreams, and songs—and know that every word, every note, and every rhythm is important.

Now it's time to dive in. Use the pages ahead to write down your songs, experiment with new ideas, and discover just how creative you can be. Remember, the best songs come from the heart—so let your imagination guide you, and have fun making music!

Let's Start Writing!

Celebration & Reflection

Congratulations! You've done something truly amazing—you've written your own songs, explored your creativity, and discovered the joy of being a songwriter. Take a moment to celebrate everything you've accomplished, because songwriting isn't easy, and you've worked hard to make something special!

Celebrate Your Songwriting Journey

Every song you've written is a piece of your own story, and each one is important. Whether you wrote a whole song, just a few lines, or experimented with different melodies and rhythms, you've taken big steps on your songwriting journey.

- **Think about how far you've come:** At the beginning of this book, you were just starting to explore songwriting. Now, you've created music from your own ideas, written lyrics that tell a story, and learned how to bring everything together with rhythm and melody.
- **Share your songs:** Your songs are meant to be heard! Share them with friends, family, or even perform them for your class or at a special event. Your voice has the power to inspire others, and your songs might be exactly what someone needs to hear.

Reflect on Your Creativity

Songwriting isn't just about the music—it's also about expressing yourself and exploring new ideas. As you look back on the songs you've written, think about what you've learned along the way:

- What was your favorite part? Was it writing lyrics, creating a melody, or finding the rhythm that made your song come alive?
- What inspired your songs? Did your songs come from a special memory, a feeling, or something from your imagination?
- How did you grow as a songwriter? Did you learn something new about music or discover a new way to express your thoughts and feelings through your songs?

Keep Writing, Keep Creating

This book is just the beginning! The more you write, the more your creativity will grow. Here are a few ideas to keep you going:

- **Keep a songwriting notebook:** Carry a small notebook with you so you can jot down song ideas, lyrics, or melodies whenever inspiration strikes.

- **Write with friends:** Working with other songwriters can be a lot of fun and can help you come up with new ideas. Try writing a song with a friend or family member!

- **Listen to all kinds of music:** Inspiration can come from anywhere, so listen to different styles of music to find new sounds and ideas to include in your own songs.

- **Be proud of your work:** Remember, every song you write is a reflection of you, and that makes it important. Whether it's a fun song, a silly song, or a serious one, it's all about expressing yourself through music.

You Are a Songwriter!

With all the songs you've created, the ideas you've explored, and the music you've made, there's no doubt about it—you're officially a songwriter! And the best part? There are so many more songs inside of you, just waiting to be written.

Whenever you feel inspired, grab your pencil, hum a tune, and start writing again. Your next song could be your best one yet!

thank you!

A Final Thought:

Thank you for sharing your amazing talent and creativity! The songs you've written—and will write— are yours forever. No matter where your journey takes you next, your music will always be a part of you. So go out there, keep making music, and remember—your voice matters, and your songs can make the world a brighter place.

If you've enjoyed using this book, your thoughts can make a difference. Leaving a quick review not only helps us continue creating books you'll love, but it also helps other musicians, creators, and music lovers decide if this book is the right fit for them.

Scan the QR code below to leave a review.

Visit our Author Page on Amazon.com to explore our full collection of music-themed creations.

Made in the USA
Columbia, SC
04 December 2024

48390032R00059